I BANG DOWN A SILVER BELL

POEMS BY TOMMY BLAKE

Copyright © 2016 by Thomas Blake and Rich Blake

All rights reserved. No part of this book may be replicated or transmitted on any form or by any means, electronic or mechanical; including photocopying without permission in writing from the Author.

ISBN: 978-0-9984018-0-5

I Bang Down a Silver Bell/Blake-1st ed.
1. Poems. 2. Poetry. 3. Verse.
4. Blake.

Design by Tony Zajkowski

No Frills Buffalo/Amelia Press
119 Dorchester Road
Buffalo, New York 14213

For more information please visit:
www.nfbpublishing.com

For Mom

CONTENTS

Foreword

Sunshine Memories

Wildflower

A Lonely Ghost Charmer

Haze's Day and Nights at Boogy Creek

Shamrock's Tale

A Milestone of True Love

The Butterfly Circus

Florian Grimalkins

A Cobblestone Garden

Tubby Pipsy

A Rainy Eyes

The Junkyard River

All the Mid Dreams of a Journey People on an American Road

Sweet Occurrence

FOREWORD

Selecting the following fourteen poems was a simple task. No agonizing choices were made. The compilation phase amounted to inspecting a shoebox stuffed with computer print-out pages of poems that my brother Tommy had sent me over the years from his home in Daytona Beach, Florida. Every poem was included, along with a few others discovered while moving Tommy back to our hometown of Buffalo, N.Y. a few years ago.

A majority of these poems were written between 2002 and 2014, a time period that coincided with Tommy going completely deaf and then subsequently regaining his hearing via two cochlear implants — this after living his entire life being mostly deaf. Growing up, Tommy, with help from a hearing aid, barely heard, but just enough to become a tremendous lip-reader and hold his own in conversation. Completely losing his hearing, not surprisingly, caused Tommy a great deal of anguish. He went through a variety of grief stages. Acceptance was not one of them.

Tommy did his own research on a procedure that was rarely considered to be an option for his situation (deafness associated with cerebral palsy). But he made it clear to us siblings, particularly to our sister, Patsy, that he wanted to explore it. He underwent three brain surgeries in five years. By 2009, Tommy was truly hearing sounds for the first time in his life — a church choir, the rush of a creek, the clip-clop of a trotting horse, The Who's "Tommy."

What began as a way for me to keep a long-standing promise to my brother evolved into an undeniable realization: Tommy Blake is my favorite poet of all time. His style is surreal, naturally so. I'll concede here that I have scant knowledge of, or appreciation for, poetry. Sure, I enjoy Edgar Allan Poe's "The Raven" and at one time I was into Jim Morrison's spoken-word stuff but that was mainly during a Doors phase in my sophomore year of college. These days, I do, yes, occasionally read poetry. That's mainly because each week a neighbor in my apartment building leaves her spent New Yorker magazine on a stairwell window ledge. It usually goes unclaimed, thus affording me access to at least a couple of poems per week — so let's just say I've perused ten exceptional poems per year, for at least ten years. And I can't recall ever enjoying any of these verses, exquisitely crafted, but entirely unmemorable. Tommy's poems are different. They take up residence in your craw. They linger a while and tickle your imagination.

Tommy had demanded to hear, so it's fitting, indeed, that his literary voice demands to be heard.

With a profound ambivalence, Tommy flouts grammatical rules, creating his own unique tone, his language, stark, vivid, if at times abrupt. His themes are far-reaching and universal. Nostalgia for family, patriotism, love, war, peace and nature intermingle with ghosts, freaks and psychedelic imagery.

One of Tommy's oldest childhood pals, John Gallivan, was given an advance copy of *I Bang Down a Silver Bell* and, after devouring it, he texted me a stab at a book jacket "blurb."

His rather apt synopsis: "Beautiful and baffling. . . Tommy has touched the feet of the saints."

Rich Blake
November 9, 2016

Sunshine Memories

Sometimes my parents used to shun the wicked ways
Ol' sunshine memories fade away

The homestead of poor people listened to an old radio show called
The Shadow
Ol' sunshine memories fade away

The poor boys and girls poured down the bucket of water on
sizzling summer days
Ol' sunshine memories hung on

I know grandma gone into October skies
The grandfather on my mother's nest loved to eat a mashed potatoes
The grandfather passed away into a summer breezes
The grandfather came as the pride of a working man
The grandfather on my father's home love a good Irish jigs
My grandfather slept into a winter sun

A timeless dove flopped in a dew light
A shamrock of luck gave a pair of bundle to the heartdroppers

On the shore, I'm only a son of a American soldier who fought for his
beloved country
My parents were exhale their lung for a flaming desire

I believe it wasn't me to burn a sore heart

Ol' sunshine memories plunged on a lake Erie

Ol' sunshine memories flew on a ashful of snow

That's all began with my mother

My mother proclaimed as a nurse to nurturing the heal-less patients, pale full of human faces

Ol' sunshine memories hang on

My oldest brother sat on a high tide to striving to cling on a stable road

Ol' sunshine memories dancing into a youthful night

My older brother had a ton of daring
He stepped to brought his freedom rides
My brother bedazzled as a U.S. Marine
And dashed as a financial planner

My sister in law flows as a flawless mother in the family

Ol' sunshine memories fling away

My older sister wore a white coat
She sang a happy song as a dentist

I bang down a silver bell at Buffalo River
Ol' sunshine memories sting on

I wasn't a mighty rock to hit a summer parade

I woke up as a shocking bolt at Children's Hospital

I was born deaf and a wobbly legs

I couldn't hear the word of hate

My younger brother became a razzling writer
Bleeding away for a penniless dream

My youngest brother couldn't believe
In the darkness of God
Slamming as a brazen railroad man

I couldn't hear a sparkling sound of my family

My family sprinkled the seeds of a green grass

Ol' sunshine memories stoked at tudor boulevard garden

Weary-less dream

Ol' sunshine memories dance away

Dancing to a youthful night

Ol' sunshine memories hang on

Wildflower

A ocean tide raving against the rock

A brave one saving the French poodle on the boat

A Vietcong find the real address of Marlon Brando

A wildflower convert into shady lamp

Everlasting. Oh peace never die

A mild wind lie down the mean street

A Lonely Ghost Charmer

The skeleton was laughing about the wishbones
The darkness was glooming across the night sky
The bats slaughtering the fleshes of sparrow
The butcher dragged the body of deer
The ghost dancer is clapping his soul to erase the evil spirit as the cool breezes
Flowing along the palm trees

The wily scarecrow is singing in his wicker chair
Mr. Lanier Hox didn't seem to bother to turn off the t.v.
Folklore tales was the sudden impact to the ghost dancer

Oh! Mr. Lanier Hox gave the motel key to the vampire teenager
The ghost dancer dashes around near the boggy pond
A fulsome of music chilled the unspoken children

The ghost dancer hugged in a passionate force to all people
The golden plate shines from a lawnmoter
The ghost dancer jabbing at a shaken old man
The pipeline flushes out a ton of water
Mr. Lanier Hox plunged to swim to cling the white rock

The axe-man slashes the fragment of the body into ashes
The ghost dancer has a bittersweet feeling for the meekness of people
The crimson moon motel was vacant for a long duration
The ghost dancer was Mr. Lanier Hox

Oh! Mr. Lanier Hox never debunking a true love to anybody
Mr. Lanier Hox walked down the road to say

"So long for now."

Haze's Day and Nights at Boogy Creek

Upon a life itself
A grey Pelican snap the post
A sizzling air boils at a dog named Mervie

A summer of blue love

A jazzy music paces the human organ's spirit. A soggy night flew the woman's pew. Hey! Huey splashes his dove soap. Oh! Say you spoken an unbroken dream
The last time cloverfleaf camp.
The dampness of rain never harm a innocent ones

Shamrock's Tale

A deaf boy rushing down the green hill

a deaf boy bleeding by a gun shot

a wolfhound dog came to believe a sound

a deaf boy pounding and pounding at shamrock

a wolfhound dog in lay lick the wounded young boy

a deaf boy cries in silence
a priest made a red stick and shout at the evildoers

a deaf boy named Shane

glory!

a evildoers ran insane

a evildoers rambled by a lawmakers

A Milestone of True Love

A lonely creature clapping down with a worn brown shoes.

A souless fellas sworn in his wicked paw

A flock of grey wolves pour their drooling lips to hear

A foes of deerslayers

A sweet dame reach out to the hares of a everlasting greeness

the jaw of a workingmen clinch their true loves

A wombats slaughtered the surface to flew their wings

A hallow of true love to a dampness field

The dove flapping their white wings to heal the unsung hero

A milestone of true love shines to the ocean and the landmarks

The hordes of a diligent forces behind their bitterness

The lame of good deeds weaves their faith to a bold causes.

The Butterfly Circus

The ringmaster shout all the freaky performers like woman with a beard and the laughing clowns jump out of a whirlpool.

The bowfin sisters share the same body.

The thin man grown a longest fingernails.

The young children were overwhelmed with unhidden sites.

The rugged man put a knife into a small ears as the lion roars to smell any meat inside the cage.

The butterfly flew through the sunflower by a lonely man with one eye.

The tiger stumbled to a bravest woman wears a black leather.

The fattest man loves to eat a hamburger.

The Chinese iron men threw a elephant to the empty room but the bubble man lives in the plastic room.

The ugliest man had a fork tongue with a needlepin.

The super diver plunged of the cannonball.

The dwarf people collect the spiders in the fish bowl.

The deaf man was hunged upside down on wire rope.

The crooked man was born as a elephant body.

The swordman chopped the rubber tires in the fastest time. The bumbling man has the most hair.

The woman was born bald and live in a swamp field.

The phony jester hopped over the silver moon.

The lovely woman has the tiniest eyes.

The juggler flopped any snakes in the air.

The crows ran on top of the tallest man who bend sideway.

The foolish man licks a thousand bees in the honey area.

The everlasting story would be a woman who has eight legs.

The blindman smokes one hundred cigarette in his mouth.

The Iraq wheelchair man dresses up as a male mermaid and loves to splash at volleyball girls.

A insane woman grew a purple beard. A little girl grew a black beard.

The stutter brothers had a longest ears.

A irate priest went outburst in tears.

Doc Yuris Yellowriver cures some of the unharmful people.

A white robot fought boxing with other robot.

A amputee sits on the stool and sung a beautiful romantic story.

Florian Grimalkins

In the green hill
Florian Grimalkins crawled
inside ancient castle

The folklore singer
likes to sing a old Irish song:
'The Irish Eyes are Smiling'

Florian ran miles
to miles
to the longest river

Shannon River

The wolfhound dog dashed to the rock

Florian hates nursing homes

The shamrock weaves back and forth
at Spanish port

The surfers waved at Mr. Florian Grimalkins
Florian was picked up by a fisherman

Some Irish people in the village likes to play a bagpipe

Pele O'Shea gave a can of tuna fish to Florian

The young boy
threw a couples of tomatoes at Florian

The fisherman yelled
at his son
Danny

Florian watches
the farmer takes care of his sheep

The rainbow appears
down on dawn street

the pot of gold was near the sea

inside the tugboat everybody ates beefstew and brown bread
the powerful storm pounds harsh
Pele searches any sign of light

The blue heron flew over
cross the bright sizzling sun

The whale trampled
a few splash

Jig dancers tapping their toes in the tugboat

Florian was born deaf mute

On Sept. 11, 2011
The two planes crashed through the twin towers
One plane ruptured the Pentagon
A another plane bejerked down on a Shankville, Pa.

Florian mourned
for the innocent victims of terrorist attacks

Florian cared about the soulful ones

Florian take the time to save a crying baby on the ground

The young mother found her beautiful baby near the tower

Florian's hair kept converting from red to green

The red hair is a signal for madness; the green color is for good love

Florian does fear
of sadness everywhere

Florian paced
to the nearest bus stop

The next journey is city of nickel is known as Buffalo, New York

Florian couldn't believe the worst snow jokes

Florian's paws was blister of warts.

The wickedness came burst of crimson smoke.

The black cat named was Timon.

Timon loves to licks
any blood
of bats

Florian

has own

free will

to plunged over the Bison river

Timon preys the pug the dog to ask for death

The dog named was Mookie a lonely creature

Florian
once again
to rescue any meekness ones

Mookie yelped
all day and night

Florian spits at Timon
With a flare of spell

Florian and Mookie
become great friends
at apple blossom yard.

A Cobblestone Garden

A white fluffy cloud leaps in the sun

A puffin sat on a granite rock

A rabbit hoppled through a green meadow

A piglet's weed sprungs up in tranquil sound

The working people stumbled near the cobblestone garden

The sunflower bursts into a exhaling by a lazy air

A rolling tides roamed into a sand

Aimlee kissed her darning innocents

A black mourning beams down at a unknown soldier's ashes

The shimming rain pours to heal the wounded causes

The warriors pinched a spiritual view

The nation of flags were strangled by a glorious fire

The freedom has a unmonotonous bells
A ibis chirped further away from the river

Tubby Pipsy

The yellow duck floating straight below the boy's stomach

The young boy makes a splash up and down in the

Center of a green giant tub.

A bubble of a mustache on a sweet creature

The mother pouted, "My dear tubby please dry off!"

The white fluffy merging into a plastic air ball

The whole room was running out of space.

The irate dog barked at the stubborn kid.

The airball just dashing through the window.

The spouted little man pacing

all around the lifeless floor

The purple furry grass was grooming on the top of the platform

The doomslayer was unspoken.

The spitting force of a undesirable food were messy

A uproaring child, "Mommy! Daddy! I'm choking into a puffy dark marshmellow monster." The journey itself was rapidly shot for a curious flyer.

The Tob Ton village was stunning.

The bouncing object foaming much thicker.

The thunderous vibration of rain

crashed into spinning nowhere

The boy was drowning into cobblestone river.
The boy was converting as a roughie fish.

The pipsy family beg farewell

A Rainy Eyes

A railroad men swiftly blew the horn

To marches the vastness of the field

The baneful setting of a home scared the farmers

The blueness of a sky

looping and looping to capture the prize of a stable rock

A irate sound decay through the coal miners

and yelping to merge the fire.

A beacon glow upon the empty fences to combine the soulseekers

The preacher repeatly shaken the vow of a rainy eyes clutches to the workingpeople.

The shine of soft cloud drip down at a fisherman

 scorned the rule of a seafare by a captain

The captain of a tugboat glancing at a fulsome creature to uprising the chopping surface of a ugly storm.

The railroadmen edge the track

To hunch their peril of a wrathful forces

The flippant banker

Debunking the law of a working crowds

The poor people hoodwinked any unspoken voices to shun the unjustice to their land

The monotonous chill

Damped the spirit of a pride and joy from the unsung heroes

The grimness of a rainy eyes

Belongs to the diligent folks

The drunkard spitting and spitting

As a rainy eyes to bow at a wooden cross

The victory in the air toppled to a fallen shallow to a lowly hearts.

The land shines through the truthfulness of a blue coller

The soldiers salute the wounded warriors

To nurture the causes

Of a freedom befitted as a glorious drumbeat

The Junkyard River

The prune river flows across the smokehouse. The cooker named was Arlan Norwich and he loved to flip a t-bone steak with his family, two girls dancing around the broken mirror.

The mother held her small bell and shout, "Tracie, Jobeth, dinner is ready." The elder mother pacing to hear her name, Dotty, by the horn.

The silver pan hung on the wooden fence. The python snake was crawling inside the toilet. The yellow daisies blooming over crack cement.

The chainsaw flopped over the lofty chair outside the Norwich home. The vernom chirping to the surface of the grass. The young boys were throwing the golf bags in the junkyard river.
The old men were debunking the wasteful creatures. The stallion horses roaming to the piles of hays. The devil flaming out of his mouth. The yellow striped cats ran furious to hide their fears.

The derelict likes to sleep on the mattress. The hazy air sizzles and boiling toward the water pump. The wishing well occurs to be as a empty hole.

The three hungry dogs yelping to obey on the junkyard river.

The banjo players were exhaling their lungs and sung of the old sunshine memories.

The soul healer collecting any sound of seashells. The frog leaping on the lily pad. The ailing turtles flapping and churning near the fish bowl.

The cubs was spinning the small rocks. Mama bear was taking the black cubs to the sand box.

The bumbling bees sting Tracie and Jobeth Norwich's ears.

The poor deaf mother makes a sign language for help.

The warmhearting moment was evening shade for the Norwich family.

The junkyard river calmly fade away.

The gold diggers got themselves a handful of

Floating treasures boxes.

All the Mid Dreams of a Journey People on an American Road

Crashing through the sand
A violent warrior
The roaring of thunderous fires crashing in the city of Baghdad
A wounded cry vibrates to the eyes of our American soldiers
The lonesome dove holds a green leaf sat on a crimson rock.
The flock of innocent people exhale their lungs.
In Washington, D.C., immigrants all over the globe are chanting for peace.
A rugged homeless has a collection of medals in a shoebox.
The wildest dream couldn't fade away.
The white mourning of cloud beaming cross the golden bridge.
The journey workers
Have a huge hope to dig the oil
in Alice, Texas
The souls of the our military officers took a train
To observe the vastness of heartland.

The young
And the old
Parents are dancing
For a glorious victory
From South Carolina

The American flag strained
To behold the fullest freedom
The common men
And women
Are waving their small flags
To be in the center
Of a sport stadium
The battlefield

Awestrucks the hordes of our humble farmers
In Kansas City, Missouri

The rumbles of patriotic riders
Roaming along
The American road

Sweet Occurrence

A lonely dancer
likes to pass a day
of a dozen roses
everywhere

A lonely dancer composed his feet
on the wooden floor

The cardboard moon
swings
back
and forth.

The female clown
appears
with orange hair
and wears
a purple suit

The clown named Daisy.
Daisy blew many kisses
to the innocent ones.

The angels flew
all over town
the town of Tarry Town

The starry night shines
through the circus tent
Daisy plunges
into a small barrel.

Everyone was cheering
and laughing
at the female clown.

The horses rushed through
around in circles

The tallest man
walks

and
played
a flute

As the cowboys
and indians
firing their guns in the air

Midgets threw chocolate
M&M candies
To the crowds

The tigers were roaming
around in their cages
and the monkeys
were climbing the ropes.

The fattest woman smiles
At the ringmaster

Miss Daisy was speechless.

She had to use sign language. The circus people had to travel many miles by train to cross the heart land of America. The farmers salute all the performers at Mums field, Kansas. Miss Daisy enjoyed giving hugs to everyone.

The young lovers sat down to watch the circus
Miss Daisy was just an old lady with big baggage. Male clown was tickling Daisy all the time.

Terry the old clown never retires as a circus performer

The ring master shouts

HAPPY VALENTINE'S DAY!

The children were dancing
with a lonely dancer.

The military officers came to watch
All the circus performers

The opera singer liked to exhale at the tent

The strongest man holds up
the stone of heart

The fastest woman
hop on a stallion horse

And the magician
plopped up rabbit
out of a black hat

And Miss Daisy bids all the kiddies

FAREWELL!

www.ingramcontent.com/pod-product-compliance
Lightning Source LLC
Chambersburg PA
CBHW032106040426
42449CB00007B/1200